T

...o be returned on or before
...st date...

D0177899

WORLD BELIEFS AND CULTURES
Hinduism

Revised and updated

Sue Penney

H **www.heinemann.co.uk/library**
Visit our website to find out more information about Heinemann Library books.

To order:
☎ Phone 44 (0) 1865 888066
🖹 Send a fax to 44 (0) 1865 314091
💻 Visit the Heinemann Bookshop at www.heinemann.co.uk/library to browse our catalogue and order online.

First published in Great Britain by Heinemann Library, Halley Court, Jordan Hill, Oxford OX2 8EJ, part of Harcourt Education. Heinemann is a registered trademark of Harcourt Education Ltd.

© Harcourt Education Ltd 2001, 2008
The moral right of the proprietor has been asserted. Sue Penney has asserted her right under the Copyright Designs and Patents Act 1988 to be identified as the Author of this work.

All rights reserved. No part of this publication may be reproduced, stored in a retrieval system, or transmitted in any form or by any means, electronic, mechanical, photocopying, recording, or otherwise, without either the prior written permission of the publishers or a licence permitting restricted copying in the United Kingdom issued by the Copyright Licensing Agency Ltd, 90 Tottenham Court Road, London W1T 4LP (www.cla.co.uk).

Editorial: Nancy Dickmann
Design: Steve Mead and Debbie Oatley
Picture research: Melissa Allison
Production: Alison Parsons

Originated by Modern Age Repro
Printed and bound in China by Leo Paper Group

13 digit ISBN: 978 0 431 11030 1

12 11 10 09 08
10 9 8 7 6 5 4 3 2 1

British Library Cataloguing in Publication Data
Penney, Sue
Hinduism. – (World Beliefs and Cultures)
1. Hinduism – Juvenile literature
I. Title
294.5
A full catalogue record for this book is available from the British Library.

Acknowledgements
The publishers would like to thank the following for permission to reproduce photographs: Andes Press Agency/Carlos Reyes-Manzo pp. 5, 10, 16, 22, 29, 30, 35, 38; Ann and Bury Peerless pp. 7, 12, 17, 20, 37, 43; Art Directors/Helene Rogers pp. 18, 34; Christine Osborne Pictures pp. 6, 8, 9, 21, 23, 26, 36, 40, 41; Circa Photos Library pp. 11 (John Smith), 14 (Bipin J. Mistry), 25 (William Holtby), 32 (Robyn Beeche); Corbis pp. p. 39 (Bob Krist), 42 (James Leynse); Corbis/Reuters/Ajay Verma, p. 28; FLPA/E. and D. Hosking, p. 4; Hutchison pp. 24, 27, 31, 33; Mary Evans Picture Library p. 13. Background image on cover and inside book from istockphoto.com/Bart Broek.

Cover photo of a Hindu deity reproduced with permission of © Getty Images/Taxi.

Our thanks to Philip Emmett for his comments in the preparation of this book.

Every effort has been made to contact copyright holders of any material reproduced in this book. Any omissions will be rectified in subsequent printings if notice is given to the publishers.

BROMLEY COLLEGE OF FURTHER & HIGHER EDUCATION	
ACCN.	B53257
CLASSN.	294.5
CAT.	LOCN

Contents

Any words shown in bold, **like this**, are explained in the glossary.

Dates: In this book, dates are followed by the letters BCE (Before the Common Era) or CE (Common Era). This is instead of using BC (Before Christ) and AD (*Anno Domini* meaning in the year of our Lord). The date numbers are the same in both systems.

Introducing Hinduism

Hinduism is the oldest of the major religions in the world. No one really knows when Hinduism began, but it goes back at least 5000 years. It developed gradually over a period of about 1000 years, in the area that today is called northern India.

Hinduism has many different 'branches'. It is a way of life, not just a religion. Its followers have a wide range of beliefs and ways of worshipping. Different Hindus may believe quite different things without anyone saying that they are right or wrong.

Hindus often use the image of a banyan tree to explain what their religion is like. A banyan tree is a sort of fig tree which grows in India. It is very strong, and its branches spread out in all directions. The branches send roots to the ground and the new roots then help to nourish the tree. Hindus say this is like their religion – it spreads in all directions and draws from many different roots, but its origins come from one trunk.

Hinduism is often compared to the spreading roots of the banyan tree like the one above.

Sanatan dharma

Hindus do not usually use the word 'Hinduism'. They describe what they believe as **Sanatan dharma**, which means '**eternal** truths'. Hindus believe that their religion follows basic teachings that have always been true and always will be. These truths are written down in the Hindu holy books. Hindus believe that the whole universe and everything in it follows these eternal truths. Most Hindus are not particularly interested in converting other people to follow their beliefs.

What do Hindus believe?

Hinduism teaches that there is one Great Power called **Brahman**. One translation for Brahman is 'ultimate reality'. While some people see Brahman as somewhat similar to the Western term 'God', it is not quite the same thing. Hindus believe that Brahman is everywhere and in everything. Nothing would exist as it is if Brahman was not in it. They often use the illustration of salt water to explain this. The salt cannot be seen, but it is present in even the tiniest drop of the water, and without it the water would be quite different. In the same way, Brahman is present in everything in the universe, and makes everything what it is.

Most Hindus say that the Great Power can be seen most easily through gods and goddesses. Two of the main gods are Shiva and Vishnu. There are important goddesses, too. Durga and Kali are fierce and frightening, Parvati and Lakshmi bring peace and good fortune. Many of the gods appear in different forms to describe different aspects of their personality. This can be very confusing, even for Hindus. However, most Hindus agree that all the gods and goddesses are different ways of describing the Great Power, Brahman.

Reincarnation

Belief in rebirth, or **reincarnation** affects every part of a Hindu's life. Reincarnation is the belief that when you die your soul moves on to another body. This may be another person, or an animal or a plant, as Hindus believe that the soul in everything is the same. Where your soul goes depends on how you have lived in this life. The aim of every Hindu is to break out of this cycle, so that when they die their soul can become part of Brahman. This is called **moksha** and will be a state of perfect happiness.

Hindus worshipping at a temple in the UK.

Hinduism fact check

- ◆ Hinduism began in India more than 5000 years ago.
- ◆ There have been many important leaders and teachers in Hinduism, but Hindus do not follow the teachings of any one person.
- ◆ Hindus worship in temples. They also have **shrines** at home.
- ◆ Hindus worship Brahman through gods and goddesses. Images (**murtis**) represent different aspects of the power of Brahman. They are treated with great respect, as if they were the god or goddess themselves.
- ◆ The oldest of the Hindu holy books are called the **Vedas**.
- ◆ About 830 million people in India are Hindu, and Hindus live in many other countries of the world. There are about 1.4 million Hindus in the United States, about 600,000 in the United Kingdom and about 95,000 in Australia.
- ◆ The symbol used for Hinduism is made up of **Sanskrit** letters. (Sanskrit is a very old language, in which the Hindu holy books were first written.) The letters spell the word **Aum** (pronounced Ah-oo-m).

Hindu gods and goddesses

No one knows how many gods and goddesses there are in Hinduism. Some people say that there are thousands, some people say millions. Most Hindus believe the gods and goddesses are **symbols** or ways of describing Brahman, the Great Power. Hindus believe Brahman cannot be described, and can never be understood. They believe they are more likely to worship Brahman properly if they worship through a god or goddess they can understand. There are many stories about the gods and goddesses. Hindus believe these help people to learn about themselves and life in general. The stories describe the gods' families, and their good and bad tempers and feelings, just as if they were ordinary people.

Lakshmi, goddess of beauty and wealth, with Ganesha. He has the head of an elephant, and is the god of wisdom and good fortune.

Gods

Hindus believe that three gods make up the 'trimurti', or 'three forms'. These are Brahma the creator, Vishnu the preserver and Shiva the destroyer. These three work together to maintain the cycle of life in the universe. Everything is made, lasts for a time and is then destroyed so new things can be made. Brahma is not worshipped very much today, but Vishnu and Shiva are both popular gods. Ganesha, Shiva's son, is also worshipped regularly today.

Vishnu

Vishnu is worshipped under several names, because Hindus believe he has come to earth in several different forms, called **avatars**. The stories say that if the world is in great danger, Vishnu comes to protect it. This has happened nine times. The two most important avatars were the gods Rama and Krishna.

Shiva

About a quarter of all Hindus worship Shiva. He can be frightening because he is the destroyer, but he can also be kind and easy to please. In statues, Shiva is often dancing the dance of the universe – the movement which keeps the whole universe in motion.

A legend about Vishnu

Manu, the father of the world, was bathing in the river one day when a tiny fish begged to be rescued, because bigger fish wanted to eat him. Manu took the fish home and dug a pond for him to live in. The fish grew and grew, and eventually asked Manu to put him in the ocean. As Manu let him go, the fish warned him that there was going to be a great flood and Manu should build a boat to save himself. Manu did so, and the flood came. During the storm, the fish appeared again as a huge creature with golden scales and a horn. He caught hold of the ship's anchor rope and pulled it along for many years, until they came to rest on top of Mount Hemavat, which was still above the water. Manu anchored the ship there to wait for the end of the flood. Before he left, the fish told Manu that he was really Vishnu, and Manu had been saved so that the world would not be entirely destroyed.

Ganesha

In the god-family, Ganesha (pronounced Ganesh) is the son of Shiva and the goddess Parvati. In a temper, Shiva cut off his son's head by mistake. Ganesha's head was replaced with an elephant's head. Ganesha is often worshipped today, because he is the god of wisdom and good fortune. Hindus setting out on a journey or starting something new often pray to Ganesha, and his image is often buried in the foundations of a new building.

Goddesses

The mother goddess is Shiva's wife. She has several names. As Durga, she is supposed to destroy demons. As Kali, she is frightening, but she is thought to bring peace of mind to the people who worship her, because she helps them overcome their fears. She is usually shown with a necklace of skulls around her neck, and holding weapons in her six or eight hands. The mother goddess also has a gentle side. As Parvati she is peace-loving, and as Saraswati she is the goddess of music and learning.

A murti (image) of the mother goddess Kali, who helps people overcome their fears.

Lakshmi

Lakshmi is Vishnu's wife. She is the goddess of beauty and good fortune. She is often pictured standing on a lotus flower. Many Hindus pray to her at the festival of Divali, which begins the financial year. They hope she will help them to prosper in the year ahead. Lakshmi is thought of as a wanderer, who never stays long with anyone.

The history of Hinduism

The Great Bath at Mohenjo-Daro, part of the Indus Valley civilization that flourished around 2500 BCE, in what is now Pakistan.

You can find the places mentioned in this book on the map on page 44.

Hinduism was not founded by one person, or group of people. The religion developed gradually over a long period of time. It started so long ago that no one really knows how it happened. The history of Hinduism and the history of India are closely connected. Today, about 80 per cent of the population of India – about 830 million people – are Hindus.

The very beginning

The beginnings of Hinduism can be traced back to a very ancient civilization which flourished in the Indus Valley between about 3000 and 1700 BCE. In the twentieth century archaeologists discovered some of the remains of this civilization, and proved that the people had a very organized lifestyle. They also found statues which show that the people worshipped a mother goddess and a bull. The remains of a huge bathing area show that bathing was an important part of their worship.

In around 1500 BCE, the region was invaded by people called **Aryans**, who worshipped gods of the sun, moon and stars (nature gods). It seems that over many years the two forms of worship came together. People probably carried on worshipping their own gods,

Hare Krishna

There are many different groups in Hinduism. They usually follow the teachings of a particular holy man, often called a **guru** or swami. One of the most well-known groups of Hindus in Western countries is the International Society for Krishna Consciousness (ISKCON). This was begun by Bhaktivedanta Swami Prabhupada in the 1960s. His teachings are based on those of a Hindu holy man who lived in the sixteenth century CE. These say that people are not really 'alive', but are 'sleeping' and do not understand the real meaning of life. They need to 'wake up' to their real selves. They can do this by repeating a **mantra** or prayer, Hare Krishna. Hare means 'God who forgives wrong-doings'. People who belong to ISKCON are strict vegetarians. They live simple lives, believing that everything they do is an offering to the god Krishna.

but they began to worship other gods, too. From about 1200 BCE, the Aryans composed special hymns to the gods. These were called **Vedas**, so this period of the Hindu religion is called the Vedic period.

The early days of Hinduism

The people of India probably carried on worshipping in very similar ways for about a thousand years. Then, gradually, some people became dissatisfied. They began to look at the teachings of other religions. In the fourth and third centuries BCE, the teachings of the Buddha Gotama became popular. The **Buddhist** Emperor Asoka, who ruled most of India, encouraged the people of India to follow the teachings of the Buddha. By the end of his reign in 232 BCE, almost the whole of India was Buddhist.

Hindu leaders realized that this was a serious challenge for Hinduism. It had to become more organized and ideas began to change. People began to worship Shiva and Vishnu, rather than the nature gods they had been worshipping before. Worship of the gods in temples became less important as people began to worship more at home. This meant people were more likely to worship one god who was particularly important to them, rather than many gods equally.

The Puranic period

The Puranic period lasted from about the fourth to the thirteenth century CE. The name comes from the **Puranas**, important stories that were written down during that period. This was also the time when Hindu teachers began to put together some of the ideas and teachings of Hinduism which are still important today.

Between the twelfth and sixteenth centuries CE, India was invaded three times by different groups of Moghuls, who were **Muslims**. During this time Hinduism became less popular again. While some Moghul rulers were tolerant of Hindus, others did not agree with Hindu ways of worship, and many Hindu temples were destroyed.

The past 200 years

During the past 200 years, the world has changed very rapidly. Hindu leaders have worked to make sure that Hindu beliefs stay constant. In the nineteenth century, a teacher called Vivekananda worked to present Hinduism as a world religion for the first time. In the twentieth and early twenty-first centuries, Hinduism has developed in many countries as Hindus have travelled to different parts of the world.

A festival procession by members of ISKCON in London, UK.

The origins of the caste system

The **caste** system is the way that Indian society has worked for hundreds – probably thousands – of years. It divides people into groups. There is a story in the Rig Veda about how the caste system began. It says that the first man was called Purusha. He was sacrificed by the gods, and…

> *into how many parts was he divided? What did his mouth, arms, thighs and feet represent? The* **Brahmin** *was his mouth, the* **Kshatriya** *his arms, the* **Vaishyas** *his thighs and the* **Shudras** *were born from his feet.* (Rig Veda 10.90.12)

Religion divided society into four groups or **varnas**. The first and most important varna, called Brahmins, were priests. The second varna, Kshatriyas, were soldiers. The people who ruled the country came from this group. The Vaishyas were shop-keepers, traders and farmers. The last of the four groups were the Shudras, who were servants for the other three varnas. Over many years, these varnas divided into many smaller groups called **jatis**. A person's jati was decided by what job their family did. Jobs were passed on in families, so a son would do the same job as his father. Girls in those days did not work outside the home. Today, it is no longer the case that sons or daughters must do the same job as their parents, because people have more educational opportunities and usually more freedom of choice. However, they still stay in the same jati. People in some jatis are thought to be more pure (closer to God) than those in others.

A Hindu priest distributing prashad (sacred food) at the end of worship.

Harijans

Outside the four varnas were the **Harijans**. They did the dirtiest jobs. For example, many Harijans worked with leather, which other Hindus would not do. For many years, other Hindus shunned Harijans. The Hindu leader Mahatma Gandhi worked hard to improve the lives of these people. He used the term Harijan, which means 'child of God'. Some members of this group actually prefer to use the term Dalit, which means 'oppressed'.

The caste system today

The people in India have lived under the caste system for hundreds of years. In the past 50 years, things have changed. More people travel away from their home area, to live and work in cities. In factories and shops they have to meet and talk with people who are not

In many Indian villages people live in a very traditional way.

Niranjan's view

Niranjan is 13 and lives in London, UK. There are lots of Hindus near where we live and a lot of families belong to the same jati. Back in India years ago all my family were farmers, but my grandfather came to Britain, and my father worked very hard to get lots of qualifications. Now he is a doctor at a hospital in London. About 20 years ago, people from the jati clubbed together and bought a church hall that wasn't being used any more. I go there on Saturday mornings for the classes so that I can learn to read and write Urdu, which is what we speak at home. The adults use the hall for lots of other things as well – there's a group for old people, and I go to the youth club on a Friday sometimes. It's good to meet other people who are brought up in the same way as me.

from their own varna. They cannot keep the rules so strictly. Now many Brahmins are not priests, not all members of the army are Kshatriyas and many people who are not Vaishyas own shops. Apart from Brahmins and Harijans, many people are not sure which varna they belong to, although they know what jati they are, and what this means in their dealings with other people.

The law has changed too. Partly because of the work done by Mahatma Gandhi (see page 13), laws were passed to try to make Indian society more equal. However, it takes a long time to change the way people think, and changing the law is not always enough. In many villages in India the caste system is still very strict. This means that people will not marry someone from a 'lower' jati, and anything they eat must have been prepared by someone from their own or a 'higher' jati.

Shankara (788–820 CE)

Shankara was born into a family of Brahmins (priests) and became a holy man when he was quite young. He gave up his home and his family, and spent the rest of his life travelling around India, teaching. He founded temples in many different parts of India, and his beliefs and teachings attracted many followers.

Shankara's teaching was about the relationship between the soul which Hindus believe is in everything – **atman** – and the Great Power, Brahman. He taught that atman and Brahman are the same. They only seem to be different because human beings cannot understand Brahman. This means that only Brahman is real. Everything in the world only seems to be real. Shankara often used an example to illustrate this:

> *A man goes into a dark room and sees a rope on the floor. He thinks it is a snake. For that man, the rope really is a snake until he discovers it is not.*

Shankara taught that the way human beings see the world is the way the man sees the snake. Shankara's ideas are the foundation of a large part of Hindu teaching.

A statue of Ramakrishna at his birthplace in Bengal, India.

Ramakrishna (1834–86 CE)

Ramakrishna was a great leader of Hinduism in the nineteenth century. He played a major part in reviving Hinduism and making it more structured. He came from a poor family and, at the age of 21, he became a priest at the temple of the goddess Kali, near Calcutta, in India. He became so involved in the worship that he often used to go into deep trances, becoming unconscious to everything around him. His holiness and the way he cared for people made him very famous, and many of his followers believed that he was an avatar (human form) of the god Vishnu.

When he died, he left behind many followers who continued his work. One of them was Vivekananda, who worked to present Hinduism as a world religion for the first time.

Grief for Gandhi

When Gandhi was killed, the Indian Prime Minister, Jawaharlal Nehru, made a radio broadcast. This is part of what he said:

'The light has gone out of our lives and there is darkness everywhere. Our beloved leader, Bapu, as we called him, the father of the nation, is no more. The light has gone out, I said, and yet I was wrong. For the light that shone in this country was no ordinary light. In a thousand years that light will still be seen ... for it represented the living, the eternal truths, reminding us of the right path, drawing us from error, taking this ancient country to freedom.'

Mahatma Gandhi (1865–1948 CE)

Mohandas Karamchand Gandhi was one of the most important Hindus of the twentieth century. He was born in India but trained in England as a lawyer. He began work in South Africa. There, he became aware of racial **discrimination**, and he became well known as a writer and fighter for freedom. As a Hindu he believed that all life is sacred, and this gave him the basis for his way of fighting. He insisted that protesters did not need to use violence. Throughout his life he taught the idea of **ahimsa** – non-violence and respect for life.

In 1915 Gandhi returned to India and became an important national leader. During the 1930s, he played a large part in the negotiations for independence as India left the British Empire. As part of the independence settlement, the new country of Pakistan was created to be a Muslim country. In what is thought to be one of the largest movements of people in history, six and half million Muslims moved to Pakistan, and over five million Hindus moved from Pakistan to India.

Encouraging the use of the spinning wheel was part of Gandhi's peaceful way to gain Indian independence from Britain.

This caused bitterness and fighting, and thousands of people were killed in riots. Gandhi used all his influence to calm the fighting, even going on hunger strike and risking his own life to persuade people to stop. In January 1948, Gandhi was shot dead by Nathuram Godse, a member of an extreme group which disagreed with Gandhi's teachings. Over three million people took part in his funeral procession, and he is remembered and respected as a man of peace by people all over the world. The title Mahatma means 'great soul', and is a way of saying that by his example he showed how love can overcome evil.

Hindu holy books

Hinduism has developed over about 5000 years. In that time, hundreds of different Hindu holy books have been written. Some praise the gods, some outline and describe the correct ways of worship. Some put forward and discuss Hindu beliefs. Most of these books were written in Sanskrit, which is one of the oldest languages in the world. Today Sanskrit is not spoken anywhere, and it is only used for religious purposes. Some of these holy books are not often read now, but others are still very important.

The Hindu holy books are divided into two main groups. Some are called **shruti**, which means 'heard'. Hindus believe that these words were heard by wise men in the early days of the religion. Others are called **smriti**, which means 'remembered'. These are words that were handed down by word of mouth for hundreds of years before they were written down. A father would teach his son the words, the son would teach his own son, and so on. People in those days were used to remembering things, because very few people could read or write.

A priest reading the Vedas at home in front of his shrine.

The two main groups of shruti texts are the Vedas and the Upanishads.

The Vedas

The Vedas are the oldest of the Hindu holy books. Hindus believe that the Vedas are not of human origin, and they contain basic truths which never change. Veda means knowledge or wisdom. The words the Vedas contain go back to about 1200 BCE, but they were not collected together and written down until about 1400 CE. The most important Veda is the first. It is called the Rig Veda, and contains over 1000 hymns, made up of verses called mantras. The hymns are really poems praising the 33 gods who control the forces of nature, the gods of the Aryan people. The other Vedas contain instructions to the priests about how worship should be carried out, and descriptions of religious ceremonies. This is part of a hymn to the earth goddess, Prithivi:

You send us the water-laden cloud, O shining goddess. With your strength you hold the trees firmly in the ground when the lightning flashes and thunder-rain showers from the sky. (Rig Veda 5.84.3)

The Upanishads

The Upanishads are the last part of each Veda. The name comes from words which mean 'sit down near', and this is how the teachings began. Young men who wanted to learn from the older, wise teachers would sit down around them, listening to what they were saying and learning from it. The Upanishads contain discussions about the most important things that Hindus believe, for example, what Brahman is like, and about the soul in all things, atman. The Upanishads were written down between about 400 and 200 BCE. Other holy books are of the smriti group.

The Laws of Manu

The books of the Laws of Manu are some of the most important law books for Hindus. No one really knows when Manu lived, but his words were written down by 300 CE. There are 2685 verses in the Laws of Manu. They contain instructions about how Hindus should live their lives, and show how important it is to follow the teachings of Hinduism in everyday life. They include the punishments for certain crimes, and rules which priests should follow. The Laws of Manu are very detailed, for example:

No guest should be allowed to stay in a Brahmin's house without receiving hospitality, food, water and a bed.

The Puranas

The Puranas were written down over a period of about 1000 years, after about 500 CE. Puranas means 'olden times'. They are part of the group of holy books which help to explain the Vedas. They contain many well-known stories, and deal mainly with the worship of Brahma, Vishnu, Shiva and Shakti. Altogether there are over half a million verses in the Puranas.

Prayers from the Vedas

Hearing the words of the holy books is still very important to many Hindus, even though they are now written down in books. One of the prayers in the Rig Veda is to Savitiri, the sun god. Many Hindus repeat this prayer every morning as part of their worship. It is known as the Gayatri mantra (or prayer).

In Sanskrit this prayer looks like this, and the translation is written below.

ॐ भूर्भुवः स्वः । ॐ तत्सवितुर्वरेण्यं भर्गो देवस्य धीमहि । धियो यो नः प्रचोदयात्

We meditate on the loving light of the god Savitri. May his brilliance, like that of the sun, stimulate our thoughts.

The smriti

Hindus believe that the shruti (heard) holy books contain teachings that were revealed to holy men, as well as their ideas and thoughts after they had spent years studying the religion. Ordinary people found them difficult to understand, so other traditions grew up. These were based on the same sort of teaching as the holy books, but were in the form of stories which were easier to understand. In time, the stories themselves became part of the smriti (remembered) holy books. Among the most important part of the smriti are two long poems. One is called the Mahabharata, the other is called the Ramayana. They contain stories which Hindus of all ages love to listen to. They also teach lessons about the religion.

Dances of the stories from the holy books are popular.

The Mahabharata

The Mahabharata is the longest poem in the world. It has 100,000 verses! It was written by many different people over several hundred years. The poem is complicated, because as well as the main story it has many other stories which are included to teach important lessons. The main story is about two royal families. They are cousins, and quarrel over who should be the rightful ruler of the country. One family tricks the other, and war begins. There is a great battle. Before the battle begins, one of the royal princes, Arjuna, talks to the person who is driving his chariot. This person turns out to be the god Krishna in disguise. This is the most famous part of the poem, and it includes the Bhagavad Gita, probably the best-loved part of all the Hindu holy books.

Bhagavad Gita means 'song of the Lord'. It deals with some of the most difficult teachings of the Hindu holy books, but in a way that is easy

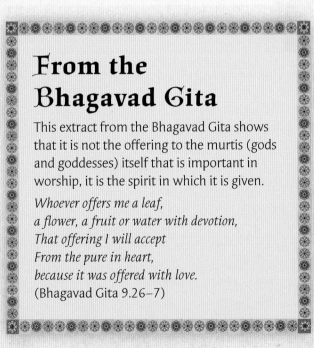

From the Bhagavad Gita

This extract from the Bhagavad Gita shows that it is not the offering to the murtis (gods and goddesses) itself that is important in worship, it is the spirit in which it is given.

Whoever offers me a leaf,
a flower, a fruit or water with devotion,
That offering I will accept
From the pure in heart,
because it was offered with love.
(Bhagavad Gita 9.26–7)

to understand and that all Hindus can relate to, wherever and whenever they live. For many Hindus, the Bhagavad Gita is the most important part of the holy books. In the story, Arjuna tells Krishna that he does not want to fight, because the battle is against his cousins, and he does not want to kill his relations. Krishna teaches the prince about his duty and about the right ways for people to worship.

The Ramayana

The Ramayana is shorter than the Mahabharata, but it still contains 24,000 verses. It is thought to be the work of a man called Valmiki, and was probably written down about 100 CE. It is divided into seven books, in which the main character, Rama, is an avatar (human form) of the god Vishnu. The characters are all 'ideal' – in other words, they are either all good or all bad. Prince Rama is a good son, a loving husband, a wise king. His wife Sita is beautiful, modest and obedient to her husband. The demon Ravana is totally bad.

Stories in the Ramayana

In the story of the Ramayana, Rama's father promises his youngest wife two wishes. She asks for her own son, Bhavata, to be made king instead of Rama, and for Rama to be sent away for fourteen years. The king is heartbroken, but must keep his promise to his wife. Rama obeys his father and goes to live in a far-off country, with his wife and his brother. One day, while Rama and his brother are out hunting, Rama's wife Sita is kidnapped by the wicked demon Ravana. He keeps her prisoner on an island. The monkey-god Hanuman helps Rama to find Sita, and Hanuman's monkey army helps Rama to attack the island. They win a fierce battle against Ravana, in which Ravana is killed. Rama and Sita are able to return home. Rama is crowned king and everything ends happily. Good wins over evil.

An old painting showing a scene from the Ramayana (notice Rama and Sita, seated, and Hanuman kneeling).

The stories in the Mahabharata and the Ramayana can be understood in many different ways. For children, they are exciting stories. For adults, they can be understood on a much deeper level, teaching important lessons about the gods and the way to worship. Hindu actors and dancers often use the stories in their performances, because they are familiar to almost everyone.

Worship at home

What Hindus believe about worship

Hindus believe that Brahman is in everything. This means that every part of life can be part of worship if you do things carefully and with thought. Even everyday tasks such as cooking or cleaning can be part of worship if they are done with the right attitude and in the right way. Hindus also worship in special ways in temples and at home. This worship may include **meditation**, or repeating the names of God. It may include reading or listening to readings from the holy books. The most common form of worship is called **puja**. This means making offerings to the murtis in the shrine, a holy place.

This family are worshipping at their shrine. Notice this shrine has a picture of Ganesha.

Shrines in the home

Hindus normally have a shrine in their home, where they worship at least once a day. Shrines can be quite different, depending on what the family can afford. In some houses, the shrine room may be separate and beautifully decorated. In other houses, the shrine is a simple cupboard or shelf. Like the gifts offered to the murtis in worship, it is not the size or appearance of the shrine that matters, it is the spirit in which it is used. The most usual place to find a shrine is in part of the kitchen or the mother's bedroom.

The most important thing in a shrine is the murti, the image of a god or goddess. Sometimes there are pictures of other gods or goddesses, too. The shrine always has perfume and flowers, so that the murti and the pictures are in beautiful surroundings. Some shrines have a little bottle containing water from the River Ganga (Ganges) in India, which Hindus believe is a sacred river.

What happens in worship?

The rules about making puja, or worship, are written down in the Hindu holy books. At home, puja is often performed by the wife or mother in the family. She prepares for it carefully, often bathing and wearing clean clothes. Hindus believe that the murti in the shrine represents Brahman, so they treat it very carefully. During puja it is washed and dried, and may be touched with coloured powders. Sometimes flowers are hung around it. Small gifts such as a flower petal or a grain of rice are offered. It is not the size of the gift which is important, it is the love with which the gift is offered which really matters.

Part of the puja is repeating mantras. A mantra is usually a verse from one of the holy books. Mantras begin with the sacred Hindu word Aum. Sometimes Aum is used on its own as a mantra, too. The mantras are repeated over and over again. Hindus believe that this is a way to help them concentrate on God.

Puja usually takes place in the morning and evening. In many Western countries, where the adults in the family may have to leave early every morning for work, evening worship is more usual. Whilst they are making puja, Hindus do not wear shoes. They sit cross-legged on the floor, or stand up. They often put their hands together and lift them to their face or in front of their chest. Sometimes they kneel and touch the ground with their forehead. These are all ways of showing respect.

This girl is worshipping Krishna at the shrine in her home. Notice that the murti is blue, a colour which Hindus believe is a symbol of holiness.

Radha's view

Radha is 13, and lives with her family near New York, USA. This is how she describes worship at their family shrine.

In our house, we worship God through Ganesha. Hindus always pray to him before we go on a journey, and before we start anything new. Every morning, we have a bath and then all sit cross-legged on the floor in front of the shrine – Mom, me and my brothers Rama and Anil. On a weekend Dad is there too. Mom washes the murti of Ganesha by sprinkling milk mixed with water over it, and dries it by stroking it with cotton wool. She dips more cotton wool in sandalwood paste and in perfume and pats the image. Then she puts a small garland of flowers round its neck. We say prayers and leave little gifts in front of the image. I like the feeling that starting the day with worship gives me. When I get to school, I feel more confident about tackling new things – even in math! – because I know that Ganesha helps people to succeed.

Hindu temples

There are thousands of temples in India. Some are like small villages, with lots of different buildings. Others are tiny shrines by the side of the road. Hindus believe that the variety of shrines is a way of showing that Brahman is everywhere, and can be seen in many different ways. In Western countries, Hindu temples are often buildings that were originally used for other purposes. More purpose-built temples are being built as Hindu communities become more settled in local areas. Sometimes a temple is called a **mandir**, which is a **Gujerati** word.

In India, worshipping at a roadside shrine is part of everyday life.

Where are temples built?

Many important temples are built where stories say an event happened in the life of a god. The place became a centre of pilgrimage, so a temple was needed. Small roadside temples were often built to remember an event, or to ask a god's protection for travellers. A water supply is important, partly because people need water to wash themselves before they can worship. Also, many Hindu gods are associated with water, and water plays an important part in the religion.

Symbols in a temple

Temples include many objects which are symbols. Many temples fly a flag outside, which is a symbol of the presence of Brahman. Temples often include a tower as part of the building. This is a symbol of the pillar which people in olden days thought was at the centre of the universe. A person going to the temple to worship goes from the outside to the shrine room, often in the centre of the building. This is a symbol of the spiritual journey which a person makes in their life – the journey which Hindus believe leads to moksha, freedom from the cycle of birth and death. When Hindus go to worship in a temple, they take off their shoes before they go inside to show their respect for the murtis. They may also ring a bell as a symbol of 'waking up' the god.

Carvings

Many temples are beautifully carved, inside and out. The carvings often show scenes from the life of the god. The temple doorway is often 'guarded' by frightening creatures. Most of the gods have animals which are used for transport, and sometimes the appropriate animal is included in the carvings near the doorway, so that it is ready to take the god or goddess wherever he or she wants to go.

Inside a temple

The rooms inside a temple depend on when and where it was built. A tiny shrine by the side of the road only has space for the murti and a few symbolic objects. The huge temples which have a large staff have rooms where they can live, as well as many different shrine rooms so that different murtis can be worshipped.

At the entrance to a temple there is always a place where worshippers can leave their shoes. Everyone going to worship removes their shoes as a mark of respect, as well as to keep the holy place clean. The main room is the shrine room, which is always at the heart of the building. This is usually carpeted and is beautifully decorated with paintings and statues.

Especially in Western countries, the temple is an important focus of life for Hindus. If the building is large enough, the temple has other rooms which help it to serve as a community centre. Toddler and pensioner groups may meet there, as well as youth clubs. Some larger temples have a hall where marriages can be performed.

The symbol for Aum at the feet of a murti (image) can become part of worship.

The Aum signal

The most important sound for Hindus is the word Aum (also spelled Om). It is pronounced as if it was written ah-oo-m. For Hindus, this is a holy sound because it represents the sound of the universe (ॐ). They also believe that it is the origin of all sound. Aum begins and ends all prayers, mantras and the **bhajans** (hymns) which are used in worship in a temple. The Mandukya Upanishad begins with the words, 'Everything is Aum. The past, the present and the future, and that which is outside time. Everything is Aum.' The symbol is often used in temple carvings and in articles used in worship.

Arti is a special part of worship in a temple.

Worship in a temple

Hindus believe that the entire universe is a place of worship. Temples are seen as somewhere special where a god can be visited – a kind of house where a god or gods live. They regard going to the temple to worship in much the same way as people think of going to visit a friend at their home.

Some smaller temples have only one murti. In large temples, the main shrine has the murti of the god to whom the temple is dedicated. Other shrines are homes for the other murtis. The murtis need priests to look after them, so a temple always has at least one priest. A priest who leads worship is called a **pujari**. A priest who also offers advice to the people has the title **pandit**. Most temples have at least one room where the priest lives. A river or other supply of water is needed, so people can perform the ritual washing before they worship.

How do Hindus worship?

Worship in a temple often begins before dawn. The worship centres around the murti, which is treated as a very respected guest or royalty. The murti is 'woken up' by the priest, and prayers are said, beginning with the sacred word Aum. The murti is washed in milk or water and dried. It may have sandalwood or turmeric paste put on it. It is dressed in red and gold clothes and has garlands of flowers placed around its neck. In some larger temples, the murti is put away at night in a separate 'bedroom', so it needs to be moved back to the main shrine room in the morning. Hindus believe that even the least important murti should be worshipped at least once a day. More important murtis are worshipped several times a day.

After all the preparations are complete, the priest who leads the worship draws back the curtains. Hindus believe that this not only means that they can see the murti, but that they can be 'seen' by the deity. This is a very special moment which Hindus call **darshan**.

The five lights of the arti ceremony

The five flames on the arti tray are symbols. They represent the five elements of nature, which are necessary for human beings to survive. These are water, fire, earth, air and space. The number five also symbolizes the five senses that human beings have – sight, smell, taste, hearing and touch. It is a way of saying that people should love and worship Brahman with their whole being.

The arti ceremony

During the **arti** ceremony, the priest lights five lamps in a steel tray. For each murti, he moves the tray in a clockwise circle from the bottom to the top of the murti. Then it is circled again from left to right. As he is doing this, the worshippers sing a special song and chant a prayer.

The priest then circles the arti tray in the direction of the three other walls of the temple, a way of worshipping the gods who are the guardians of the four main points of the compass. He sprinkles water over the worshippers, often from a special shell. This is a symbol to show that the blessings of Brahman are being given to them. The arti tray is carried around among the people who are worshipping. Sometimes they put small gifts of money on the tray. They hold their hands over the flames, and then move the palms of their hands over their eyes, forehead and head. They believe that by doing this they receive power from the god. During the worship, **prashad** is distributed to the people. This is food which has been blessed by the god. Usually it consists of nuts, fruit and sweets.

People who are worshipping may place a dot or stripes of special powder or paste on their forehead. This is usually made of sandalwood or turmeric and is called **tilak**. It is a symbol of the soul which is within everyone. The shape of the tilak shows which god the person has worshipped. A similar mark is made by the pujari on the forehead of the murti. Tilak is not the same as the red dot which many Indian women wear on their forehead, which shows they are married.

A young Nepalese girl receiving tilak, a symbol or mark which shows she has been to worship.

The Pashupatinath temple, Nepal

For Hindus who worship Shiva, Pashupatinath is one of the most important centres of **pilgrimage** in Asia. Thousands of Hindus go there for the Mahashivaratri celebrations in the month of Phalguna (see page 34). Because it is so important, the Pashupatinath temple, unlike most Hindu temples, is closed to non-Hindus.

Worshippers at the Pashupatinath temple, Nepal. Notice the cremation ghats at the side of the river.

The temple stands on the banks of the River Bagmati, a sacred river, about 5 kilometres (3 miles) outside Kathmandu, the capital of Nepal. The buildings there date from the seventeenth century CE, and the site was used for worship for hundreds of years before that. Alongside the river are many **ghats** or platforms, used for people to bathe and for **cremations**. The ghats closest to the front of the temple are only used for royal cremations.

You can find the places mentioned in this book on the map on page 44.

The central temple has three roofs, which are covered in gold. Around them are several other buildings used by worshippers and the priests who live in the temple. There are many other smaller temples in the grounds of the main building. The grounds are dotted with stone columns, called **linga**, which are symbols of Shiva.

How Shiva saved the world

The gods and demons wanted to be able to live for ever. Vishnu told them that they must obtain a liquid called the nectar of immortality from the celestial ocean of milk. To do this they had to churn up the milk, so that it would give up its treasures. They began to churn, using the great serpent Vasuki as a churning rod. They churned and churned for a hundred years. The first gift that the ocean gave them was the goddess Lakshmi, carried out of the milk on a bed of lotus flowers. Other gifts followed. Then, as they churned, the great serpent began to spew out a deadly venom. He had a thousand mouths, and all of them began pouring a poison that would kill everything that lived. Shiva leaped forward and swallowed the poison. He was so powerful that it could not harm him, but swallowing it stained his throat dark blue. By this act, he saved the entire world from extinction.

Stories and legends like this help Hindus to understand the important teachings of their religion, and so help them worship at home and in temples all over the world. This story also explains why murtis which show Shiva as a person (rather than the linga, which is his usual symbol – see page 34) show him with a blue throat.

The Shri Swaminarayan temple, Neasden, London, UK

This modern temple was completed in 1995. It was inspired by the man his followers call His Divine Holiness Pramukh Swami Maharaj. He is the leader of a group of Hindus who follow the teachings of Lord Swaminarayan. The temple is the largest outside India, and is the first traditional stone temple to be built in Europe.

The stone for the temple – over 2800 tonnes of it – came from Bulgaria, and 2000 tonnes of marble came from Italy. This was all shipped to India to be carved in the traditional ways before being brought to London and put together like a jigsaw puzzle. In planning the temple, the architects took into account Hindu teachings on respect for life. Materials and furnishings were chosen for their environmental friendliness, and the heating and lighting systems are energy-efficient. For example, because 226 English oak trees were felled and used in the building, 2300 oak saplings were planted in the UK and India.

The temple has five beautifully carved shrines for the murtis. The prayer hall (the largest in the world to be built in the past hundred years) is where the arti ceremonies and prayer meetings take place, five times each day. However, the temple is not just a centre for worship. There is a visitors' centre with an exhibition about Hinduism. The buildings also include rooms which can be used for meetings, educational activities and other events, and a marriage hall. There is also a purpose-built sports hall, which was included with the idea that 'if the young come to play they will in time come to pray'.

The Swaminarayan temple in London, UK, is the largest Hindu temple outside India.

Pilgrimage

You can find the places mentioned in this book on the map on page 44.

A pilgrimage is a journey which someone makes because of their religion. Many Hindus believe that making a pilgrimage is part of their religious duty. They may want to ask for something special, or give thanks for something good that has happened to them. They may want to visit a place where the god they worship appeared to people, or where a miracle happened. Most Hindus believe that by going on pilgrimage to a special place, they will achieve better karma. **Karma** is the belief that actions from previous lives affect this life and future lives. Good actions in this life will help a person to be reborn to a better life next time.

Places for pilgrimage

There are hundreds of places for pilgrimage all over India, visited at any one time by thousands of pilgrims. There are 24 main temples in India, of which twelve are more important than the others. Four of these twelve are the most important of all. They are thousands of kilometres apart at the four 'corners' of India. Puri is on the east coast, Dwarka is on the west coast and Badrinath is in the far north of India: these are shrines to Vishnu. Rameshwaram on the south coast is a shrine to Shiva.

Many Hindus spend most of their lives saving up to be able to visit all four of these temples. They may be poor and have great difficulties on the journey, but they believe that putting up with the hardships is part of serving Brahman. For this reason, some Hindus believe that a pilgrimage has more value if the pilgrim walks to the shrine. This may mean a walk of hundreds of kilometres, taking weeks or months, but they believe that the effort makes the pilgrimage more worthwhile. When they arrive at the temple or shrine, many pilgrims crawl around it on their hands and knees. This is a symbol that they are sorry for the wrong things they have done in their life.

Worshippers at the temple at Puri on the east coast of India.

Worship

When they arrive at the shrine, the worship is of a similar pattern to worship anywhere else. At the popular shrines, hundreds of people may queue for hours to gain darshan – the view of the murti. The offerings they give to the god they have come to worship are the same sorts of offering they would give in worship at home – food, flowers, money.

Holy rivers

Water is necessary for life, and Hindus believe that rivers are a symbol of Brahman who gives life. Bathing in a holy river is a symbol of inner cleansing – washing away **sin**. There are seven holy rivers in India, but the most famous is the River Ganga (Ganges).

Varanasi

The most important place on the River Ganga is Varanasi, sometimes called Benares. This is where the

A holy man bathing at the source of the River Ganga, in India.

god Shiva is believed to have lived, and it is has been a centre for Hindu teaching for thousands of years. On the banks of the river are special platforms called ghats with steps which allow pilgrims to reach the river to bathe or offer puja. Every Hindu hopes to be in Varanasi when they die, and some of the ghats are used for cremating dead bodies. After the body has been burned, the ashes are scattered in the River Ganga. The ashes of people who have died elsewhere are often scattered there, too. Hindus believe that this will help the person to achieve moksha, breaking out of the cycle of rebirth.

The River Ganga (Ganges)

The River Ganga flows from the Himalayas to the Bay of Bengal, and is 2510 km (1560 miles) long. It is not the longest or the largest river in India, but Hindus believe that it is the most sacred river in the world and they treat it as the goddess Ganga come to earth. The source of the river is called the Cow's Mouth. It flows out of an ice-field almost 400 metres (over a thousand feet) high, and begins as a river almost 30 metres (100 feet) across. Along the length of the river, and especially at Hardwar, Allahabad and Varanasi, millions of Hindus bathe in its waters. They believe that drinking even one drop of its water will get rid of all the sins they have committed in this life and in previous lives.

Celebrations

Lighting candles is part of the Divali celebrations.

Hindus celebrate many festivals throughout the year. For most Hindus, Divali is the most important festival in the year. It takes place at the end of the month of Ashwin, and carries on into the month of Kartik (October – November in the Western calendar). Not all Hindus celebrate Divali in the same way. Even in India, customs can very greatly. Celebrations in other countries can be quite different again. In some places it is a three-day festival, but it usually lasts for five days. Divali includes the beginning of the financial year.

Divas

Throughout the festival, Hindus decorate their homes, temples and other buildings with rows of lights. In the past, small clay lamps called **divas** were used. Divali is a short form of the word Deepavali, which means 'rows of lights'. Today, small electric lights like fairy lights are often used instead of lamps. Glitter and tinsel are often used for decorations as well.

Yamu's view

Yamu is 12 and lives with her parents, grandparents, cousins and their parents in Bombay, India. On the first day of Divali, we light a single clay lamp. This flame is for Yama, the spirit of death. Sometimes we have a few firecrackers or sparklers that night but the main festival begins the next day. We all get up early and wash and put on new clothes, before we make puja at home. This second day is called Naraka-chaturdashi and we remember Vishnu's victory over the evil Naraka-Asura. On the third day we make special offerings to Lakshmi. My cousin Sita and I draw patterns called rangolis in coloured powder on the floor, and in the evening we make special puja. All the doors are open so that Lakshmi can come in, and after puja we set off fireworks to frighten away evil spirits. On the fourth day, married women get presents from their husbands. Last year my father bought my mother a beautiful red **sari** with a matching blouse piece. I think the best day is the fifth, which we call sister's day. Sita and I make a fuss of our brothers and help cook special foods for them, then in the evening they give us presents.

Stories of Divali

Divali is a special time for remembering Lakshmi, the goddess who brings good fortune. She is supposed to visit houses which are clean and tidy, and some people believe that the divas and other decorations are to light the way and welcome her to the house. Lakshmi is the goddess of wealth. Hindus hope that by welcoming her they will have a prosperous new year, as she leaves her wealth wherever she goes. Divali comes at the end of the financial year, so people who own shops and businesses make sure that their account books are up to date and that all their debts are paid. Divali is a time for closing personal 'accounts', too – for example, making up any quarrels or arguments they may have had. This means that everyone can make a fresh start for the new year and hope that, with Lakshmi's help, it will be a good one.

Lakshmi is the goddess who brings good fortune.

Another story told at Divali is from the Ramayana and is about how Prince Rama won the battle against the evil Ravana and his army, and found and rescued his wife Sita. They returned home and Rama was crowned king. The people of the country were delighted to see the popular prince return, and lamps were lit to line the streets for Rama's victory procession.

There are also stories about how the god Vishnu won a battle with a wicked giant called Naraka-Asura. In another story, Vishnu outwitted a very powerful king named Bali. In different parts of India, people think that some of these stories are more important than others. The stories are remembered in the celebrations, so this explains why the festival is celebrated differently in different areas.

Divali is a family festival. People give each other presents, and share meals with friends and relations. Sending cards for Divali is becoming more popular, especially with Hindus who live in Western countries. There are firework displays and bonfires, with singing and dancing. The idea is to show that darkness can be driven away by light. This is a symbol which shows that evil can be driven away by good.

Navaratri

Navaratri takes place in the month of Ashwin (September – October in the Western calendar), just after the monsoon rains. Its name means 'nine-nights', the length of the festival. Celebrations take place among Hindus all over the world, and Navaratri has different names in different places. In Gujerat (western India) it is called Navaratri. In eastern India, it is called Durga-puja. In northern India, the whole festival lasts an extra day and is called Dassehra. As with other Hindu festivals, different groups of Hindus remember different stories in their celebrations. Most of the celebrations honour the mother goddess. She has several different names. In this festival she is worshipped as Durga, a fierce soldier riding into battle on a lion.

Dancing at the festival of Navaratri.

Anyone who worships Durga as their special goddess keeps the festival with great care. Although fierce, Durga is also thought to care for people, so she is the symbol of mothers. In the story of the Ramayana, Prince Rama prays to Durga for help when his wife Sita has been captured. Navaratri is an important time for families. In particular, girls who have been married during the past year try to return home. They are given presents.

In northern India there are open-air plays during the festival, acting out parts of the Ramayana story. In other places, people dance round a shrine of Durga, sometimes specially built for the festival. It is a box with a cone-shaped top, and has pictures of the different appearances of the goddess on each side. The two traditional dances are a circle dance called garba and a dance with sticks, called dandya ras. People dance and sing hymns to the goddess, and festivities go on well into the night. Some people manage to do this every night for nine nights! Hindus believe that the festival is a time when they are given energy from the goddess, which they can use to make sure that they overcome the evil they meet in their own lives. At the end of each night of the festival there is an arti ceremony, and prashad (food which has been blessed) is shared.

Taking the murti of Durga to the river to be washed.

Dassehra

Dassehra means 'tenth day'. It falls on the day after the end of Navaratri. It is also known as Vijaya Dasami, which means 'the tenth day of victory'. During Navaratri, Hindus worship God through a murti of Durga. At Dassehra this murti is taken to the nearest river and washed. Hindus believe that as it disappears under the water it takes all their unhappiness and bad luck with it, and the river washes it all away. This makes Dassehra a very happy festival.

Durga and Mahishi

This is a story about Durga which Hindus remember at Navaratri.

Once there was a buffalo demon called Mahishi. He thought he could do anything he liked, because Brahma, the creator god, had promised him that he could only be killed by a woman. Mahishi was so conceited that he did not think any woman would ever be strong enough to kill him. The other gods begged Shiva to help. The goddess Durga agreed to the battle, and was armed with special weapons by the gods. Mahishi laughed when he saw her, but as she killed some of his demons, he knew he was really in danger. He changed into his buffalo form and charged her, but she was not hurt. Then, as he turned back into his demon form, Durga stabbed him with a spear. Mahishi was dead! Good had triumphed over evil, again!

At Dassehra Hindus also remember the story of the battle between Prince Rama and the wicked Ravana. Rama won the battle with the help of his brother Lakshmana and Hanuman the monkey-god, after he had prayed to Durga for help. In many places, statues of Ravana are burned on bonfires. In New Delhi, the capital of India, there is an enormous firework display at Dassehra. Wooden statues, 30 metres (98 feet) high, of Ravana and his two brothers are packed with fireworks and burned.

In all Hindu festivals, there is a serious lesson behind all the enjoyment. The story of the Ramayana is the story of how good wins over the powers of evil, and reminds people of Brahman's love. During Dassehra, Hindus try to make up any quarrels they may have had during the past year.

31

Holi

Holi is a spring festival. It is celebrated by Hindus all over the world, although they remember different stories in their celebrations. It takes place in the spring – February or March in the Western calendar, Phalguna in the main Indian calendar.

The stories that Hindus tell most often at Holi are about Krishna. When he was young he often used to play tricks on people, so Holi is a time for practical jokes. In Hindu countries everyone joins in the fun – a favourite trick with children is to throw coloured powders and water over people in the streets. There are often water-fights as people join in. In countries where most people are not Hindu, children cannot usually 'attack' people in the streets, but water-fights among children are common. The custom remembers Krishna's friendship with some milkmaids (called gopis), and the story of how his favourite, Radha, once threw coloured dye over him when they had gone out for a walk. The story has a religious meaning, because it shows how well Krishna and Radha got on together, so it reminds people that they must have a close and loving relationship with Brahman.

A procession celebrating Holi – notice the coloured powder everywhere.

Where the name comes from

A more serious story gives the festival its name. Once there was a king who was very full of his own importance. He demanded that all his people should worship him like a god. His own son, who was called Prahlada, was a devoted worshipper of Vishnu. He knew that his father was not a god, and it would be wrong to worship him. The wicked king was very angry when Prahlada refused to worship him, and he ordered that Prahlada should be thrown into a pit full of poisonous snakes. Everyone expected him to die, but Vishnu protected him and he was unharmed. Next his father arranged for Prahlada to be trampled on by a herd of elephants while he was asleep. Again, Vishnu protected him and he was not harmed.

Then the king asked for the help of his equally wicked sister, Holika. She had magical powers, which meant she would not be harmed by fire. She took Prahlada with her onto the top of a huge bonfire, expecting him to be burned to a frazzle. Instead, Prahlada chanted the names of Brahman over and over again, and Vishnu protected him. Holika did not know that her magic powers only worked when she was in the fire alone, so they vanished and she disappeared into the flames. The lesson of the story is that Prahlada who trusted Brahman was saved, but Holika, who thought she had powers of her own, was destroyed. Holika gives the festival its name.

To remember this story, many Hindus celebrate Holi with a huge bonfire. Mothers sometimes carry their babies around this bonfire in a clockwise direction, as a symbol that they hope Agni, the god of fire, will bless the baby with a long and happy life. It is a custom to heat coconuts next to the fire, and then eat them.

Raksha Bandhan

Raksha Bandhan is a popular festival which takes place on the day of the full moon in Shravan (July or August in the Western calendar). It celebrates the relationship between brothers and sisters. Raksha means 'protection', Bandhan means 'tie'. At Raksha Bandhan, a girl ties a coloured silk or cotton bracelet called a rakhi around her brother's wrist. As she does so, she says a short prayer that he will be blessed in the year ahead. Then she gives him a sweet. In return, the brother gives her a gift and promises to look after her and protect her. If a girl does not have a brother, it is usual for a cousin to be given the rakhi, instead.

Indra and Bali

The custom of giving a rakhi comes from a story about the god Indra. He had been fighting with a wicked demon king called Bali, and had lost the battle. Bali had driven Indra out of his kingdom. Indra's wife was most upset about this, and she went to ask the god Vishnu if he would help. Vishnu gave her a bracelet made of cotton threads to tie around Indra's wrist. The bracelet had special powers and, when Indra next fought with Bali, it protected him. He won the battle and was able to drive Bali out and win back his kingdom.

At the festival of Raksha Bandhan, a girl ties a bracelet round her brother's wrist to celebrate the relationship between brothers and sisters.

Other festivals

There are Hindu festivals throughout the year. Some people say that every day, there is a Hindu festival somewhere! Most festivals involve making special puja. Some festivals are important in a particular area, or to worshippers of a particular god.

Mahashivaratri

Mahashivaratri is a solemn festival in honour of Shiva. It takes place on the night of the new moon in Phalguna (January–February in the Western calendar). Mahashivaratri means 'great night of Shiva'. Hindus believe that on this night Shiva performs a special dance that provides the energy which keeps the universe moving – it destroys, but this means that new things can be created. Dancing Shiva is called Shiva Nataraja – Shiva the Lord of the Dance.

In Hindu art, the god Shiva is often shown dancing.

During the festival, murtis of Shiva are given special attention. Shiva murtis often show him dancing, and he is often shown holding his trident – a three-pronged spear. Shiva also has three horizontal lines across his forehead, and his followers have these placed on their foreheads, too, as a sign that they worship him. A symbol of Shiva is the linga, a stone column, and Hindus pour milk over this as part of the ceremony.

Ramnavami

Ramnavami is the birthday festival of the god Rama, and takes place in spring. Rama, the hero of the Ramayana poem, is a very popular god for Hindus. He is often worshipped at the shrines in people's homes but, if they can, Hindus go to the mandir for Ramnavami to worship there, too. There are readings from parts of the Ramayana. A special part of the worship is the singing of the Ramanama, which is a list of all the names of Rama. An image of the baby Rama is placed in a cradle in the mandir. It is kept covered until midday, when Rama is said to have been born. In some places in India, the celebrations include images of Rama and his wife Sita being carried in procession through the village.

Like many other Hindu festivals, Ramnavami is a day of fasting. Fasting often means eating and drinking nothing, but for Hindus it means going without certain foods, for example, meat, fish, onions, garlic, rice, wheat and pulses. Foods which are allowed on fast days include fresh fruit, milk and **ghee** (clarified butter). These are foods which many poor Hindu families could not normally afford, so eating them is a way of making festivals more special.

Janmashtami

Janmashtami takes place in Shravan, and usually falls in August in the Western calendar. It celebrates the birthday of the god Krishna. The stories say that he was born at midnight, so many Hindus spend all night in the temple. They sing hymns in praise of Krishna, and there is dancing. At midnight, everyone gathers in front of the cradle which holds an image of Krishna. They perform the arti ceremony, then share prashad – gifts of fruit and specially-cooked sweets which they believe have been blessed by the god. A traditional drink called charnamrit is a mixture of milk, yoghurt, sugar, water and honey.

In many temples, non-stop repeated readings of the Bhagavad Gita are organized for the eight days and nights before the festival. It takes about three hours to read the Bhagavad Gita all the way through. People take it in turns, with reserves in case anyone is ill. The readings are timed to finish at midnight on Krishna's birthday.

The Shiva linga

This is the story of how the linga became a symbol of the greatness of Shiva.

One day, when the world was young, the gods Brahma and Vishnu were having an argument about which of them was the greater. Suddenly a column of light appeared in front of them. They decided to settle the argument by having a race to see who could reach the end of the column first. Brahma turned himself into a goose. He flew high up in the sky, but he could not find the end of the column. Vishnu turned himself into a boar, nosing deep into the earth to find the other end. He did not succeed either. Then a booming voice said, 'I am the Lord Shiva! You will never find my beginning or my end, because I am so great!' Brahma and Vishnu forgot their argument, and began to worship Shiva.

Decorations for Janmashtami – the festival celebrating the birth of Krishna.

Family occasions

Samskars

Special ceremonies are performed throughout a Hindu's life. These are called **samskars**. Altogether, there are sixteen samskars which should be performed at various times. Like most important Hindu ceremonies, the correct way of performing them is laid down in the holy books. The first six samskars take place during childhood.

Before birth

The first samskar takes place when a couple are hoping for a baby, before it has been conceived. They pray about the kind of child they would like. The next two samskars are performed during pregnancy. They are prayers that Brahman will protect mother and baby, so the child will be born healthy.

Birth (fourth samskar)

Straight after the birth, the baby is washed and the father or a priest places a few drops of honey and ghee in the child's mouth, using a gold ring. He says, 'May your life be as precious as gold. This will depend on your good thoughts, speech, deeds and behaviour.' Hindus make a careful note of the exact time and place of birth, which will be used by the priest who prepares the baby's **horoscope**. A horoscope is a way of telling the future based on the positions of the stars. Many Hindus use horoscopes in their life to find out the best times for events to take place.

The baby is placed in a cradle before the naming ceremony.

The naming ceremony (fifth samskar)

The baby is usually given a name when he or she is twelve days old. Hindus believe that the right name will bring the child luck. A priest is often asked to suggest a suitable initial or first syllable. The baby is dressed in new clothes and placed in a cradle. The ceremony itself is very simple. The name is announced by the eldest woman in the family, and the father says into his baby's ear, 'Now your name is ...' Everyone sings songs, and a special sweet made of fruit, nuts and sugar is given to friends and relatives who have come to the ceremony.

The next three samskars are prayers and ceremonies which take place as the baby grows. The ninth samskar takes place when the baby is about a year old, and has the first hair-cut. For a boy, this means having his whole head shaved. It is a symbol of removing any bad karma from his previous life.

Preparing a boy for the sacred thread ceremony.

The thread ceremony – upanayana (tenth samskar)

This is the tenth samskar, and is a very important ceremony for boys in the three higher varnas. Members of the lower castes do not take part in this ceremony. The boy's age may vary, but normally he is between seven and twelve. A sacred thread – a loop of cotton – is hung over his left shoulder, hanging down to his right hip. This thread is a symbol that he is joining the religion. After he has received it a boy is counted as a man. He can read the holy Vedas (see page 14) and carry out religious ceremonies. He wears the thread for the rest of his life, changing it at festivals. After the ceremony, there is a feast for family and friends, and the boy is given presents.

A guru (religious teacher) prepares the boy for this ceremony, and prays for the boy before giving him the thread. Then he becomes the boy's teacher whilst he studies the holy books. Some boys spend several years studying. The thread ceremony is thought of as a spiritual (religious) birth, so it is the reason why members of the three highest varnas are sometimes called 'twice-born'. They have had a spiritual birth as well as their birth as a baby.

The sixteen samskars

- The sixteen samskars are like markers of the stages of life (see page 39). Because the person's life is changing, they are seen as dangerous times, so the person needs the protection of special prayers.
- The first three samskars take place before birth.
- The next six take place during a baby's first year.
- The tenth and eleventh are when a boy begins his education and when he completes it.
- The next two are when a couple get engaged, and when they marry.
- The fourteenth and fifteenth are when someone retires, and when they reach the stage of giving up the world (see page 41).
- The final samskar is performed by other people, after the person has died and been cremated, when their ashes are scattered into running water.

Marriage

Hinduism teaches that marriage is important, so that there can be children to carry on the family. Sexual relationships outside of marriage are strongly disapproved of. Hindu marriages are usually 'arranged'. This mean that the parents and older relatives choose or suggest a suitable partner. Marriage is seen as joining two families, so it is important that the decision is not just left to individuals. The parents often take the advice of a priest, and may use the couple's horoscopes to make sure that they are well matched. In the past, couples did not meet until their wedding day. Now things are not usually as strict as they once were, and the young person may suggest a possible partner, or may have met the chosen partner a few times.

You can find the places mentioned in this book on the map on page 44.

The betrothal

The first step of a marriage is the ceremony to announce the engagement, or betrothal. The men from both families meet. There are readings from the Vedas, and prayers are said. The ceremony ends with a meal.

The wedding

The wedding ceremony usually lasts about an hour, but the celebrations often go on for several days. The wedding may take place in the bride's home, or a hall or the temple may be used, depending on the number of guests. The bride wears special eye make-up, and a dye made of henna is used to make patterns on her hands and feet. She wears a new red and gold sari, and lots of gold jewellery. Preparing the bride for the ceremony takes several hours. The bridegroom also offers special puja to help him to prepare for his new life. Both the bride and groom wear garlands of flowers.

An outdoor wedding in India – notice the money which has been given to the couple.

First, the bride's father welcomes the bridegroom. The bridegroom sits under a special canopy, a decorated covering. He is given small presents, which are symbols of happiness and a good life.

Then the bride arrives, usually wearing a veil so her face cannot be seen. Sometimes a veil or light curtain is held between the bride and groom. This is removed during the ceremony. The couple sit in front of a special fire which is a symbol that Brahman is present at the marriage. Their right hands are tied together and holy water is sprinkled on them when the bride's father 'gives' her to the bridegroom. There are prayers and offerings of rice.

The couple make offerings of wood, ghee and grain to Agni, the god of fire, before they walk carefully around the fire saying prayers. Then they take seven steps together near the fire. The seven steps stand for food, strength, wealth, happiness, children, the seasons and lasting friendship. At each step the couple stop and make promises to each other. While they do this, they are joined by a piece of cloth which is a symbol that they are being joined as husband and wife. Once they have taken the steps together, they are married. There are more prayers and readings, and flower petals are thrown, before the guests give their wedding presents. Then everyone shares a meal. After she is married, the bride is counted as belonging to her husband's family.

Divorce is permitted by Indian law, but strict Hindus do not accept any ending of a marriage except death. It is seen as a disgrace to both families if the couple divorce.

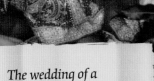

The wedding of a
Western Hindu couple.

Ashramas

According to Hindu teaching, life for males is divided into four stages called **ashramas**. When the teaching is observed strictly, the first ashrama is called the student, which begins with the sacred thread ceremony. It continues until the person is ready to set up a home and family, at which stage he should marry. This second stage is called the householder, and lasts until about the age of 50. At this age, a man is expected to leave his family and friends, and go and live in a peaceful place on his own. This stage is called the forest-dweller, and it is a preparation for the last stage, which is called the holy man. A holy man has no fixed home and as few possessions as possible. He has no responsibilities, so he is able to concentrate entirely on his religion. Today, most Hindu men do not observe these stages strictly. Young men may not be able to afford to spend ten or fifteen years studying, and many men do not want to spend the last years of their life away from their family.

Reincarnation

To understand Hindu teaching about death you need to understand reincarnation, which is an important part of Hindu belief. Reincarnation is the belief that when the body dies, the soul (Hindus call it atman) moves on to another being. Hindus believe that the atman in everything is the same – there is no difference between the atman in a plant or animal and a human being. Hindus believe that the atman goes through a series of 'steps', beginning in plants and animals, and going on to human beings. When a man or woman dies their atman is normally reborn in another person. This continual cycle of birth and death is called **samsara**.

Karma

The movement of the atman after death depends on how a person has lived. This is called the law of **karma**. Karma means 'action'. Good karma in a person's previous life will mean a good life this time. Bad karma in the previous life will mean a hard life this time. There is no idea in Hinduism of being judged by Brahman, because how you have lived will decide whether your next life is a step up or a step down. Steps may be missed, depending on the karma. Some Hindus believe that doing something very

A Hindu funeral procession in India.

The kriya ceremony

The kriya ceremony takes place ten or twelve days after a funeral. Rice and milk are made into offerings. These are not just on behalf of the person who has died, but for everyone in the family who has died in the past. Rice is an important food, and milk comes from the sacred cow. Once this ceremony has been held, the person's soul is believed to have been rehoused in another body. The days of mourning when they did not go out are over, and the family can return to normal.

bad will mean the soul is reborn in an animal, and has to work its way up to a human being again. Doing something very good may mean the soul is given a 'rest' before being reborn.

Moksha

The end of samsara is called moksha. It is what every Hindu hopes to achieve. The soul breaks out of the cycle of rebirth and joins with Brahman. Hindus say that this is like a river merging with the sea. It can only happen when the soul becomes completely pure, unaffected by anything that happens on earth. Then the soul can go back to being part of Brahman, where it began.

Scattering a relative's ashes on the River Ganga.

Hindu funerals

These beliefs mean that Hindus see death as a welcome release, because it just means leaving behind a body that is no longer needed. When someone dies, their body is washed and wrapped in a cloth called a **shroud**. A garland of flowers may be placed on the shroud, and it is put on a special stretcher. Then it is taken to be cremated on a **funeral pyre**. Where possible, this is built on a ghat (platform) by one of the sacred rivers. If there is no running water nearby, there is a cremation ground outside the town or village.

The eldest son or nearest male relative walks round the funeral pyre three times carrying a lighted torch, which sets a boundary around the pyre and is believed to encourage the soul to be released upwards into the atmosphere. Then he lights the fire. Ghee is used to help the flames burn. Families who can afford it include blocks of sweet-smelling sandalwood in the pyre. The people say prayers, and readings from the holy books remind the mourners that everyone who dies will be reborn. The closest male relative stays until the fire has gone out, then he collects the ashes. All Hindus hope that they will be in Varanasi when they die, and that their ashes will be scattered on the River Ganga. They believe that this will save them many future rebirths.

In many Indian cities, and in the West, bodies are not burned in the open air but are taken to a crematorium. Important customs like walking around the body with a lighted torch are carried out at the undertaker's. The ashes are collected after the body has been cremated. Many Hindus living in other countries have the ashes of their relatives flown back to India so that they can be scattered on the River Ganga.

What it means to be a Hindu

As individuals

Hinduism is about the way you live, but beliefs are a very individual matter. One Hindu may have quite different beliefs from another, without either being 'right' or 'wrong'. This is partly due to the Hindu belief in **dharma**, usually translated as 'duty'. Hindus believe that every person has their own dharma. It depends on the person you are, your background, the jati you belong to and many other things, so it is different for everyone. It includes worshipping Brahman, doing your best at work, not hurting other people and animals, and so on.

Worship at a temple is an important part of life for many Hindus.

The four aims of life

The first aim in life for Hindus is to do their dharma to the best of their ability. The second aim is **artha** – being able to provide for the family. The third aim is **kama** – being able to enjoy good things in life in a moderate way. When these three aims have been achieved, the fourth aim should be moksha, the freedom from rebirth which every Hindu hopes to achieve. These four aims are a very important part of life for every Hindu.

It is part of each person's dharma to choose the way in which they worship, in order to achieve moksha. The Bhagavad Gita mentions four **yogas** (paths) which people may use in their search for moksha. They are the path of knowledge, the path of meditation, the path of devotion and the path of good works. Each path is open to anyone, and Hindus do not have to choose only one – they can use any or all of them at different times in their lives. The most important thing is to reach moksha. How you get there is not really important. The most popular path is the path of good works called karma-yoga.

Respect for life

The teaching that the atman in all things is the same means that Hindus have a great respect for all living things. Because of this, many Hindus are vegetarian. In particular, no Hindu eats beef. This is because one of the things which links the whole community in

In India, cows wander where they like.

India is respect for the cow. Throughout the whole of India, the cow is holy. Cows are milked, and their dung is used as fertilizer and dried for use as fuel, but they are never harmed. They wander where they like, even in towns and cities, and there are severe penalties for killing or injuring a cow, even by accident. No one knows what this respect for the cow is based on. Some people think that it is because the white cow is a symbol of atman, the universal soul.

The Brihadaranyaka Upanishad

The fact that Hindus care for the world and the people in it is only part of their belief. The most important Hindu teaching is that there is more to living than just life, and death is not the end. A famous quotation from the Hindu holy books sums up what it means to be a Hindu:

From the unreal
lead me to the real
From the darkness
lead me to light
From death
lead me to immortality.

In the world

During the past hundred years, the movement of people around the world has meant that there are now Hindus in many countries. The teaching about dharma means they value education highly, and both men and women are to be found in professions such as teaching and medicine. Hindus living in wealthy countries are very aware of the problems faced by people in the countries which many of their families came from, and it is common for people to send money back, either to members of their family or to improve facilities for the community.

Map

The globe on the right shows the location of the map below.

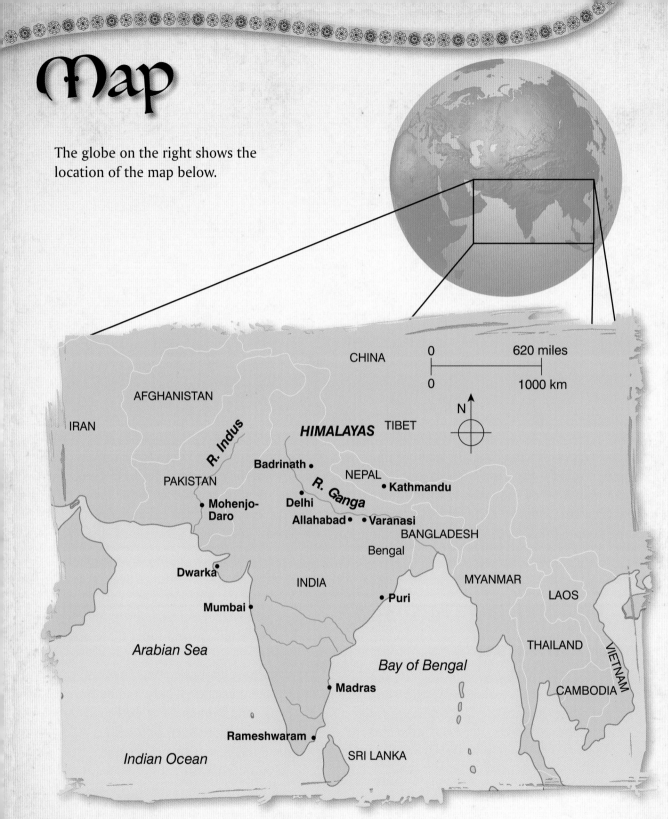

CHINA

0   620 miles

0   1000 km

AFGHANISTAN

IRAN

R. Indus

HIMALAYAS   TIBET

N

Badrinath •

NEPAL

PAKISTAN

R. Ganga

• Kathmandu

• Mohenjo-Daro

Delhi

Allahabad •   • Varanasi

BANGLADESH

Bengal

Dwarka •

INDIA

MYANMAR

LAOS

Mumbai •

• Puri

Arabian Sea

THAILAND

VIETNAM

Bay of Bengal

CAMBODIA

• Madras

Rameshwaram •

Indian Ocean

SRI LANKA

Place names

Some places on this map, or mentioned in the book, have been known by different names:

Mumbai – Bombay   River Ganga – River Ganges

Myanmar – Burma   Varanasi – Benares.

Sri Lanka – Ceylon

Timeline

Major events in world history

BCE	3000–1700	Indus valley civilization flourished
	2500	Pyramids in Egypt built
	1800	Stonehenge completed
	1220	Rameses II builds the Temple of Amon (Egypt)
	1000	Nubian Empire (countries around the Nile) – begins and lasts until c350 CE
	776	First Olympic games
	450s	Greece is a centre of art and literature under Pericles
	336–323	Conquest of Alexander the Great
	300	Mayan civilization begins
	200	Great Wall of China begun
	48	Julius Caesar becomes Roman emperor
	c4	Jesus of Nazareth born
CE	79	Eruption of Vesuvius destroys Pompeii
	161–80	'Golden Age' of the Roman Empire under Marcus Aurelius
	330	Byzantine Empire begins
	868	First printed book (China)
	c1000	Leif Ericson may have discovered America
	1066	Battle of Hastings and the Norman conquest of Britain
	1300	Ottoman Empire begins (lasts until 1922)
	1325	Aztec Empire begins (lasts until 1521)
	1400	Black Death kills one person in three throughout China, North Africa and Europe
	1452	Leonardo da Vinci born
	1492	Christopher Columbus sails to America
	1564	William Shakespeare born
	1620	Pilgrim Fathers arrive in what is now Massachusetts, USA
	1648	Taj Mahal built
	1768-71	Captain Cook sails to Australia
	1776	American Declaration of Independence
	1859	Charles Darwin publishes *Origin of Species*
	1908	Henry Ford produces the first Model T Ford car
	1914–18	World War 1
	1929	The Wall Street Crash and the Great Depression
	1939–45	World War II
	1946	First computer invented
	1953	Chemical structure of DNA discovered
	1969	First Moon landings
	1981	AIDS virus diagnosed
	1984	Scientists discover a hole in the ozone layer
	1989	Berlin Wall torn down
	1991	Break-up of the former Soviet Union
	1994	Nelson Mandela becomes President of South Africa
	1997	An adult mammal, Dolly the sheep, is cloned for the first time
	2000	Millennium celebrations take place all over the world

Major events in Hindu history

BCE	3000–1700	Indus valley civilization (worship nature gods)
	1500	Aryans invade Indus Valley (worship cosmic gods)
	1200	Beginning of the stories of the Vedas
	400–200	Upanishads written down
	c300	Mahabharata first written down
	273–232	Buddhist Emperor Asoka (Hinduism declines)
	c100	Ramayana first written down
CE	300	Laws of Manu written down
	230–480	Gupta empire (settled time for Hinduism)
	500	Puranas first written down
	788–820	Shankara (developed important Hindu teachings)
	999–1030	Mahmud of Ghazni (first Muslim ruler in India)
	1100	Ramanuja (important Hindu teacher and leader)
	1100–1500	Islamic Moghuls invade India three times, many Hindu temples destroyed
	1173–1206	Muhammad of Ghur (second Muslim ruler in India)
	1400	Vedas written down
	1526–1707	Moghul (Islamic) Empire rules India
	1834–1886	Ramakrishna (holy man and leader)
	1863–1902	Vivekananda (promoted Hinduism as a world religion)
	1869–1948	Mahatma Gandhi
	1947	Indian independence
	1958	Maharishi Mahesh Yogi founds the Transcendental Meditation movement
	1966	A. C. Bhaktivedanta Swami Prabhupada founds the International Society for Krishna Consciousness (ISKCON, called Hare Krishna)

Glossary

ahimsa	non-violence and respect for life
artha	providing for your family, the second aim in life
arti	worship of Brahman through fire
Aryans	ancient people believed to have lived between central Asia and eastern Europe in the second century BCE
ashrama	one of the four stages of life
atman	the soul which is in everything
Aum	sacred sound and symbol for Hindus
avatar	appearance of a god, especially the god Vishnu
bhajan	hymn used in worship
Brahman	Hindu name for the Great Power
Brahmin	highest of the four varnas
Buddhist	follower of the Buddha Gotama
caste	group in Indian society (see jati)
cremation	burning of a dead body
darshan	'see' – the moment of visual connection between Brahman and worshipper
dharma	'duty', the first aim in life for Hindus
discrimination	ill-treatment because of race or religion
diva	small clay lamp used at the festival of Divali
eternal	lasting for ever
funeral pyre	fire used for cremation
ghat	platform by a river used for worship or burning a dead body
ghee	clarified (heat-treated) butter
Gujerati	Indian language
guru	Hindu holy man or religious teacher
Harijan	'children of God' – lowest group in traditional Indian society
horoscope	way of telling the future, based on the position of the stars
jati	group in Indian society
kama	a regulated sense of enjoyment, the third aim in life
karma	'action' – the actions of this life which affect future lives
Kshatriya	second of the four varnas
linga	stone columns which are a symbol of Shiva
mandir	Gujerati name for a Hindu place of worship

mantra	repeated prayer, often a verse from Hindu holy books
meditation	training the mind to concentrate in a particular way
moksha	the end of the cycle of rebirth
murti	image of a god or goddess
Muslim	follower of the religion of Islam
pandit	priest who leads worship and offers advice to people
pilgrimage	journey made as part of a person's religion
prashad	food which has been blessed by a god
puja	worship
pujari	priest who leads worship in a temple
Puranas	part of the Hindu holy books
reincarnation	belief that the soul is reborn
samsara	the continual cycle of death and rebirth
samskars	the sixteen ceremonies to mark the stages of life
Sanatan dharma	eternal truths (name for Hinduism)
Sanskrit	ancient Indian language
sari	length of fabric worn as a dress
shrine	holy place often set aside for worship
shroud	cloth in which a dead body is wrapped
shruti	'heard' – name for some of the Hindu holy books containing words that were passed down before the time they were written down
Shudras	lowest of the four varnas
sin	wrong-doing
smriti	'remembered' – name for some of the Hindu holy books
symbol	expressing something important without using words
tilak	powder mark placed on the forehead to show that a Hindu has been to worship
Vaishyas	third of the four varnas
varna	a group of society; in the caste system, people are divided into four varnas
Vedas	oldest of the Hindu holy books
yoga	path – way to achieve moksha

Further Information

Hinduism, Geoff Teece (Franklin Watts, 2004)
India, Anita Roy (Raintree Publishers, 2006)
Indian Art and Culture, Jane Bingham (Raintree Publishers, 2003)
The Ramayana and Hinduism, Anita Ganeri (Evans Brothers, 2002)

Index